POST TRAUMATIC HOOD DISORDER

POST TRAUMATIC

HOOD DISORDER

POEMS **DAVID TOMAS MARTINEZ**

SARABANDE BOOKS

Louisville, KY

Library of Congress Cataloging-in-Publication Data
Names: Martinez, David Tomas, 1976–, author.
Title: Post traumatic hood disorder : poems / by David Tomas Martinez.
Description: First edition. | Louisville, KY : Sarabande Books, [2018]
Identifiers: LCCN 2017002607 (print) | LCCN 2017006886 (ebook) |
ISBN 9781946448095 (pbk. : alk. paper) | ISBN 9781946448101 (ebook)
Classification: LCC PS3613.A786424 A6 2018 (print) | LCC PS3613.A786424 (ebook) |
DDC 811/.6—dc23
LC record available at https://lccn.loc.gov/2017002607

Cover design by Kristen Radtke.
Interior by Alban Fischer.
Manufactured in Canada.
This book is printed on acid-free paper.
Sarabande Books is a nonprofit literary organization.

This project is supported in part by an award from the National Endowment for the Arts.
The Kentucky Arts Council, the state arts agency, supports Sarabande Books with state tax
dollars and federal funding from the National Endowment for the Arts.

FOR KELSY

FOR ANTHONY, ISIAH, & XOCHI

It is an absolute perfection and virtually divine to know how to enjoy our being rightfully. We seek other conditions because we do not understand the use of our own, and go outside of ourselves because we do not know what it is like inside. Yet there is no use our mounting on stilts, for on stilts we must still walk on our legs. And on the loftiest throne in the world we are still sitting only on our own rump.

—FROM MICHEL DE MONTAIGNE'S "OF EXPERIENCE,"
TRANSLATED BY DONALD M. FRAME

CONTENTS

POST TRAUMATIC HOOD DISORDER

THEY CALL HIM SCARFACE BECAUSE HE'S SAD

I knew I had gotten older
        when I noticed women no longer
                wore bras, which

didn't happen until my eyes
        began slowly lightening with wrinkles,
                though not in my eyes

        was I old,
nor could I see myself as 40
        and still in college. Yet,

there I was, and so was
        Aaliyah when she sang.

                Only in youth
        do we sing certain notes, only when
age ain't nothing but a number. I remember

                        when age's days
        felt numbered. That's when
        I got older,
                but, my family joked,
my girlfriends never did.

Now, they just want me to get a job,
then a wife.

In the movie *Scarface*, Tony Montana said
you get the money,
the power, then women. Admittedly, I'm usually

out of order. I once
went back to Cali
and came home to no
power. I called my landlord and told her
a circuit had broken;

when we discovered it hadn't, she wasn't
impressed. My first book's

initial page
is impressed. But I didn't
make any money
off that. Scratch is slang for

money, and I lament the fact
that I've never sniffed a cent

of scratch. Vaginas are considered
the original wound, and God cursed

the descendants of Eve
with painful childbirth
and menstruation
for being out of pocket.
In medieval paintings,

Jesus's wounds are often depicted
                    as little vaginas.
I have gotten
            a lot of wound.
            The etymology of vagina comes

from the idea
            of a sword being sheathed
in Latin, but also,
            in English, from the word
vanilla.
            Not from going without
            does healing come
                        but from going within.
I once spent a whole
            month in my apartment

drinking liquor
            and smelling the lingering
            smoke of my fingers.
If I hadn't already lost my job,
                        I would have lost my job.
      I cried a lot that month,
then stopped drinking,

            which made it hard to date.
            She told me
she was going to date
            and said I should too.

That's how I found out
about the great
American bra
depression

in the summer of 2015.

AND ONE

Look at the homie,
                    even when in a gang
          he came home to crack Nietzsche, *Beyond*

          Good and Evil, Will
to Power. Believing everybody dies at twenty-four,
not seeing a future in pump-faking, even then.

          You ever try to read philosophy high?
Gone to the hole and hoped for the foul,
                         wished only to finish.

After rolling joints in two Zig-Zags,
after an hour of starching pants,
he transferred trollies and buses.

                    He's going places.
Look at homie, trying to fix himself. Thinks,
out of repetition comes variation.

                    It takes a lot of effort
to look
          like you're not trying.
It should be an air ball
                    to go to college

at twenty-one, the father of two, just
to play basketball. When

most folks say they want to change the world
they mean their own.

LOVE SONG

Though I am more Che than Chavez,

                             I am still a dove.

And I do not apologize

                to you. Or to the State

of California. The IRS. New York. That administrator I bit

                in the third grade,

      who was delicious

                           and sweet.

       I, oh,

so cold.

In the mind, the Dionysian defiles walls

      the Apollonian protects.

              I am always looking

                   to take something

down. Usually it's me.

Two bulls stand on a hill. The younger says,

      Father, let's run down and fuck a cow.

           The father, wiser, longer in the horn,

      higher on the grass,

reminded his son how Moses was also horned, beamed with light,

      that to handle a massive snake,

to charm Pharaoh, to steal fire, to fly, to unzip
the sea, is to speak
and not tap vanity.

Moses descended Mount Sinai with cracked slabs
and saw a golden calf. The father said to the young bull,
No son, let's strut down and fuck them all.

Thus begins the beef between bird and bee,
the isthmus isolating
order from chaos.

My mind is made up
of so many different cuts
of meat.

At parties my favorite
icebreaker involves asking strangers
to describe themselves
with three words. Their descriptions
are a slipping
away to change clothes.

Sometimes I feel like the woman
rambling among the vapors escaping the ground
in Iceland's volcanic canyon,
making a bus

an em dash
in a rest stop,

where some fifty-odd persons
searching for themselves
            in true existentialism

                                    are yellow lupines growing
            on the side of the road. An epiphany can
            not be achieved,

                                    as a cedar waxwing
cannot be more cedar
            qua waxwing. Eventually what we're looking

for appears. Sometimes incitation opens
at the bottom of a straw, a spoon, a barrel of wine,
                        the windfall happens while eating farfalle,

                  while flipping through
                  The Autobiography of a Brown Buffalo. At the moon

      me the animal roofs
                        atop brownstones, sin vergüenza.
      Upward our eyes scamper,
                        a reflex action,
                        when inserting an object
                                    in the mouth,
even when the object
is a gun. Over

                  hills a road erodes the way home.
                        Only after the Coast Guard

                                                9

has readied a helicopter,
do we

                  descend the cold volcano in Eldgjá
to realize we are the woman

                in the search party looking
                    for ourselves.

                            to poetry.
      In moments of ecstasy

            we are lifted

At the shore of the Aegean Sea
        or at the banks

                  of the river Évros,

he loosened his sandals
        while Pegasus stamped the soil,
            crushing reeds

                  and hoofing away
      stray wood. The sun bandaged
             light on a sky

that would not heal.
      Perseus,

with eyes heavenward,
          formed the shapes of gods into clouds,

     slipped his hand
     into the woven sack,
     and felt the flint

               of primped snakes. He thought,
But it is the cold weight of scales that protects.

               As sure as a child,
he lined leaves rocked

               to sleep by salt
               water waves

     for a bed,
     so as not to,
                         with sand,
                              or with hubris,
     bruise Medusa's
               disunited head. One day,
               like a beam through skylight,

     we realize
     life is a puddle jumper of tragedy.
                         Some stones sink fast

yet still hold light. So phantom are the statues of antiquity's
          busted arms and toes, mannequins, too. I hum *You've*

lost that loving feeling, and yet still hanger hope
                              when shopping the racks of discount

          stores. Veni, vidi, vici, when I see Vince,
freeze when I see the coiled coif

                    of Versace's emblem. Like Sisyphus,
errrbody think
                    they headed for the top.

          Sing, *Started from the bottom,*
          to my reflection
                    in the dressing room mirror,

                              Now we here boy
                    when I remember

                    that
                    Oh my god, Becky, look at her butt
                    passes the Bechdel Test,
that Lawrence of Arabia runs 220 minutes
                    without one woman ever speaking.

I have eaten from the tree the fig that sullies and seen
                    that the meat's not always

                                        fair.
          I was,
               like Perseus
               and Sir Mix-A-Lot,

born by a riv

        of water,

    felled by pride when

        a brown boy, tattooed with age,

obsessed with fame, took his talents

    to Vermont to kiss trees and tap

                syrup from the sap.

      There and there

          and there, he kissed. Here and here

he drank.

        So drunk he hugged an old

           white woman

      off the ground. None of the gods

      I love

love me. To be tipsy

      is to leverage one's self.

          Or so I'm told. The pulley

is considered civilization's

        highest achievement.

           Icarus

   killed himself

     being lifted.

INCIDENTALLY

Once riding in East 619,
Heart filled, head filled with glee;
I saw an East San Diegan
Straight mad-dogging me.

Now I was twelve, no hable Español,
And he was red boned like koi,
And so I smiled, but he poked out
His tongue, and called me "white boy."

I saw the whole of East 619
From May until December;
Of all the things that happened there
That's all that I remember.

HOODIES

About suffering they were never wrong,
                  the old rappers, and though I hear

                  so many friends my age complain,
the new rappers are just
                  as burdened with wax
        and the breaks. They too fall

                for Bruegel, rock oversized
chains. Just look at "Bandz," a jam

better known by the hook, *Bandz a make her dance*,
by Juicy J, the Tennessee rapper from Triple 6 Mafia,

known for his television show,
        Adventures in Hollyhood,

        a fish-out-of-water tale
        where gangsters
        wear cowboy hats and gold teeth

and do gangster shit
        like drive golf carts with spoked rims,
        like fistfight with no shoes while getting sushi.

Who knew gangbanging
was not just a city skill but also a rural tool,

who knew how to spell Arkansas,
trepidation, gang problem, before
the *Bangin' in Little Rock* special, even if

Houston-based rapper Scarface,
            of the infamously misspelled
        Geto Boys,
                warned us that
Your hood ain't no harder than mine.

I thought of Houston as a needle
            in the haystack then, and I once met

        Scarface at an indoor swap meet in San Diego
        infamous for gang shootings,
though it would have been more aptly named

a swap meat because, there, many men and women
                traded their flesh iniquitously,
                but I should have known

Scarface was right
                because I once got in a fight
            with some dude who looked exactly like Scarface

        except not as wide or dark-skinned or really anything
vaguely similar
to Scarface,
                except that he was black,
                        and I was scared.

And that's the rub

        of the Juicy J song,

          it's easy to hear his lyrics and be blinded
by the shine of yellow diamonds and sunglasses on stage

while a teen star sits on his lap
        in a blizzard-white nightie
         singing about sexuality.

It's easy, I say, because of the beat, not to hear the wisdom
of lines like

       It's not a strip club if they ain't showing pussy
       in a world where full frontal nudity by women
is considered obscene
        yet the secret garden of so many movies.

       When it comes to contradiction, you can't counter
the dick. Not even in a movie like *Short Cuts*
        do we see anything more than The Fall,

not even when Julianne Moore's

                  bottomless,
and the ever-autumnal foliage between her hips
       burns six feet of orange,
red and yellow
            do we not miss
            the forest for the trees.

When I have drunk too much and expectation settles
across my body like a summer heat
that was so warm during the day

but so suffocating at night,
when I know no woods will stir, sometimes

I stare at my thighs with pity,
gaze at a ruler slumped
against his throne,
Hamlet, at the play's end.

I have never understood how one person could lie down
and open themselves for another,
show that even finite places carry eternity, not a heaven,
but forever. Forever is dark.

A clitoris is like a teenager with a hoodie walking down an alley.
A penis is like a teenager with a do-rag walking in an alley.
Forever is near but they won't admit it.

A poem ain't a poem if it ain't showing pussy.

TATTLETALE

Don't be a pussy
                    they said
Suck it up
                    they told me
Like a man
                    they repeated

until *walk it off, it's only
a scratch, I'll give you something
to cry about* became a simple
tourniquet. As a toddler,

stitches closed shut my scalp.
I hung from a dog's mouth,
flaccid as a rooster's wattle.
I was mauled. Still scarred by
teeth. Like any good secret,

I was carried for only so long.
Eventually after trauma
you're expected to laugh, build
a birdhouse, collect stamps.

I used to have to get drunk,
watch *Twilight* or *When Harry
Met Sally* to cry. A name

contains destiny and history.
My name means beloved
but some things can't be
loved. Liar, liar teepee

and pants on fire, all my
Yaqui beads traded. Nick
nack paddy whack, dogs
fight over the bone. *Wee wee,*
Piggy cried all the way home.

Memory nips my head. *Hush*
lil baby. What punctures child
hood quicker than being
bathroomed, whispered to
suck it.

THE/A TRAIN

A honey badger's skin can
withstand multiple blows
from machetes, arrows,
and spears, but these rusted
weapons haven't killed
anything in years, so that may
be the lesson there, that
there is no there there, like
many poems, like many
revolutions, and maybe there
isn't a there there in many
people, only that foggy
anachronistic lizard eye,
or what I have come to call
the part of consciousness
that builds impediments,
isolates, the "supertrump."
Or what New Yorkers call
subways. Or what a King
calls a dream. Or what X
called Y. What the crowd
yells as lit, the Cave calls
dim. José can you see
in West Tejas a fancy
evening out is rocking on
the porch, ain't they good
at irony, where watching

the fugitive moon runaway
takes days, like the time I
caught the C I hoped was
an A, and saw a butterfly
move in what I can only say
is protest. The wings
made small combustions
through the car. Eyes trained.
The awful is tracked by
awe. An officer lifts his
gun, yells to raise your hands
higher the TV flutters.
Watch it. They will
call you moth and kill you.

AA

the hawaiian word
for blocked lava
is aa which abandons
l & v which if o

& e double date
in english fall in
love oe in hawaiian
is you aloha means

not goodbye but love
it is suggested
that indigenous
peoples lack enzymes

to break down
alcohol but i break
down a lot i am all
about that old time

religion drinking
is a kind of blocked
lava the bourbon
cooling inside me

moving me one inch
in six hours once oh
backlit bar unkind
parthenon sacrifice

me i am a pantheon
fearing man in bed
with pillows between
her arms & legs we

slept like ellipses to
get lost in if i could
i would arrange
the stars to her

sleep i should quit
the fear of gods of
lightning bolts plagues
of being stoned turned

to spider has been
replaced love is spilt
religion i keep idols
of the old gods hidden

CONSIDER OEDIPUS' FATHER

It could have been a car door
　　　leaving that bruise,

as any mom knows,
almost anything could take an eye out,

and almost anybody could get their tongue
　　　frozen to a pole,

which is kind of funny
　　　to the point of tears
　　　plus a knee slap or two
that an eye can be made blue, pink
by a baby's fist; it fits
perfectly in the socket. It's happened to me.
　　　Get it?

Any scenario is better,
beats sitting in a car and hearing
　　　someone you love
　　　sob,
which I have done
with a black eye.

For me, a woman's tears
are IKEA instructions
on the European side.

I'm sure for Laius, Oedipus' father, it was the same.
   Think of him sleeping
after having held a crying Jocasta
because they had fought for hours
because she was stronger.

   Who knew better the anger of young Jocasta?
Knew that when the oracle or the police
      come, they are taking someone with them.

I'm sure Laius looked at the crib
      and thought, *Better you
than me, kid.*

Now consider your own
father, or the guy your mother
      dated until he took
the three-pronged road,

crouched in front of a paper
      plate with a catcher's
      mitt, teaching
      a curveball grip—

      but did he ever teach
the essential lesson
of how to block a punch
      from a finely manicured hand,
or how to walk away when
records are being candled and books disemboweled,

teach the wonderment of
        a jar of peanut butter jammed
in a TV screen
below a snail trail of ice cream
        near broken pictures on the wall?

Not while he's king, I bet, and not while
        there are mothers and their jobs,

like breastfeeding or plucking chickens,
and not while he's served a warm plate
        on a table

next
to cold beers
        from the hand

of a mother he made from a virgin
        with his own hands, his own hands.

AND TWO

extra shots. Look at homie. Out pokes
a neck tattoo. Winter couldn't possibly
                        follow fall's fallals.

Deck the halls. The oldest two-step,
dualism. Fire and Ice.

Robert means bright. Look at homie.
The Paul Atreides of
                it's complicated, wears burden

            perfectly, like a stillsuit.
Not one drop on Arrakis. Quit drinking

                but didn't stop
                popping sham
                        pain.

The homie: You need to need. Best bick back,
Young Blood. Bool it. Think you tough. Half
y'all bitch made. King Kong got nothing on
god. Don't know me, dawg. Woot. Hounds
run these Southeast Daygo streets. (Claps twice.)
Pressure bust pipes. You a sweet cake, Kool-Aid.
I'm chingon, homes. You off. I'm hood lifted.

Fuck yo couch. That rare breed. (Ring tap tap.)
Let a nine fly. You ain't talking me to death.

Barista: Yes, sir. No foam. Nonfat. Quad.

The homie: (Puts on shades.) Thank you, g.

US VS THEM

My childhood was not an anxious place,
though I lay
     in my bed, awake, thumbing
my sheets like beads, wondering when the sun
      imploded
       would Russian astronauts be OK,
they in their Sputniks, with their space dogs,
      they that chased their own tails
around this water bowl
      we call Earth. When I was a child,

in elementary school
      we practiced a type of
      protection
called Duck and Cover,
where we huddled
        under desks in case
of a Russian
nuclear attack. They were Communists,
      had the bomb, and were evil

Reagan told us
from the small grave
      of a TV screen.

In the sixties, Nixon said the same
       thing, and the Panthers
       countered with *the Viet Cong never*
called me nigger. With their picks
like unclenched fists,
       with their afros like the plumes of atom bombs,
they scared white and black folks alike. It is 2014,

and America is still afraid. Now
       the American Dream is to be debt-free,

which I am not, nor may ever be, but at least
       I'm not afraid of the Russians.

WINTER NIGHT

The late-afternoon light entered
the living room through the barred
windows like a boxer through ropes.

When my mom's bronze Chevrolet
pulled down the driveway, I hurried
away my toys. She always waved,

never smiled. Funny how my dad
coming home isn't a memory.
It was not joy when they got home

but relief. With his hand, my dad
warmed beer, and my mom, with
a fork, jabbed defrosted meat.

This was when she started calling
me Champ. At dinner, dad asked
if I wanted the belt. My memory

of those years is punch-drunk.
Her best defense was a good offense.
Like the warming before snow,

mom thawed into pleasantries.
After dinner my father sat on the floor
with his corduroy shorts riding up

his thighs while I put on boxing gloves
around his shadow. I floated, stung.
I rode his shoulders over crowds,

raised my arms. The oversized gloves
on my hands were smaller, lighter
than my want to punch him.

IN DEFENCE OF POETRY VOICE

Like a lark   lift   into moon   light.   Like   the muzzle

of a gun   I   should have raised.   Like   skirts

             over   New York vents.   Like the   joyride

in an elevator   by two   teens

with child.   Like child. Childlike. Like whining.   Like a flag

on a mailbox. Like a skateboard   off a ramp.   Like a

piano   to the   fourth   floor.   Like curtains.

Like   you   like   someone,

         not light   but deep,   so deep   light   descends

   and   when they are not in bed   you can   only   sing

to   the night,   *babe?*   Like a plague

              of toilet   paper   hung

over porches.   Like   a   brass   ring

       when   a plaster   horse   jumps.

Like   salt water. Like silicone.

Like   a chapel's   ceiling.

Like   sap seeping

    from stacked   redwood in a lumberyard.

SUPER HETEROSEXUAL ME WEARS WOMEN'S JEANS BECAUSE THE FIRST TIME

I watched porn
with other men
I was fourteen.
They were Sicilian.
They joked about
being straight
off the boat.
We would've swung
at anyone calling
our asses tushes.
In a well-lit living
room we sat
with Jesus & the
Virgin watching
us. A man &
woman squeaked
springs. Anxiously,
we breathed.
The phone
rang bareback.
The plastic
covered sofa
moaned as loudly
as we did
when the VCR
needed fixing.

With pillows
embroidered with
lilies, we
suffocated our
crotches, stopped
our leaked
electrical, until
we could not
& like French
guns, *ponf*, we
went off.

ALLEGEDLY HEMINGWAY WROTE DRUNK

Go now, and awake, children of addiction,
        believers of the bottomless,
of empty space, of empty heads, of emptiness,

the redeemers, the hoarders, the caloric counters
        of everything but the gut. Go now
eternal sleepers in the sun, rocking in the night,

sluice built throats, your own Hollywood star
        that is whiskey bottle shaped,
protectors, skinners, hiders, swallowers. Go

now, obsessed, wobbly: squint and read with one eye
        the writing on the wall.
Remember when Garamond was god, Didot an angel?

HEXAPTYCH ON AMBITION

I.

these days tongues
those pale pigs in bone fences
are so unruly
and it seems indeed that poetry
has devolved into color
books of biblical
tricks naval gazing bays
of praise swallowed
by a dark dark age
or so i hear i do not trust
any poet that did not
slurp the purple velvet
milk of excess from
lucky charms while
watching voltron
but my father says
with clear conscience
the same thing about
tang and leave it
to beaver i hear his
trepidation his fidgeting
when i play music his
point when he says
we dont come from kings
that is not why
we wear gold

his mouth is not
filled with hemlock
mine has gold
when he says *most us
just grew up poor* i too
realize that the world
odes for people
i dont like most remind
me of myself oh no
so many of them poets

II.

as in a gaggle of geese   a flamboyance of flamingoes
a brilliance   of teeth   as in a cowbell
of collective nouns   more

they call it tomming tomas
don't call me thomas myth is a
mestizo born by a tub of water
sprung from the clam fully
formed a pearl pried from the
mind of zeus inside a rooster
pecks a dinosaur which must
make me a chicken i shriek

at the armadillo of getting a
job in the smallest town of me
population one amongst cats
poetically speaking plurality
doesnt mean unity like the
naked woman dancing on
the hood of a big rig on 290
people wonder how i got here
& i fear because i am

as in a fib of poets

silly out of style the dated
mustache of neil degrasse a
bob ross afro i will never feel
popular enough loved enough

ive wished on my own star &
made myself a texas not to be
messed with been hectored
been donned been carried
been joshed been jacked asked

to get my shinebox

like a bather sunning poolside
history lies on me the moon is
half empty the night sky has
lice my hustle has been a stone
breaking the bad luck of a lake
desire the biggest circus flea
the blood thirstiest of all ticks
the heart

III.

like boobs on a bowl
of cereal buck up butter
cup you got the juice now
i hear the first billion
is the hardest boone
pickens from a plane
everything looks small
brown folks can't settle
on how colonized
they are in north america
with blankets weaved
with disease
the army did it history
is our teddy bear
cave light is very romantic
sentimentality is un
urned emotion so
many of us sacrifice
our heart to pin it down
with latin line it with
sadness to cross the heavy
heat of a stanza to be oh
the only stalk of corn
occupied with its silk
to be a chola unafraid
to tease her dyed blonde

hair to wear nike cortez
oh to be duped into
thinking youre american
oh to be eight and have
your counselor tell
your parents that if
they marked you hispanic
youd be gifted

FALLING

Nothing
   about
         wounded animals

makes me weep,

     but something about
a woman with eyelashes

     like broken wings,

     about a woman
       in red-bottomed heels
and an absent father that pulls

     the hood over my head,
     leads me

     to a stump. One.
Two. Three. Four. Five. Six.

AFTER IMAGISM

i did not learn
that love

like writing
is a twisted

game of hard
light and

clear
lines until

i was divorced
twice which doesnt

mean much unless
youve been

forced to wear black
socks embossed

with yellow tacos
a gag from a man

you were allowed
to call grandfather

for only two years
every man wants

to hear
he is grand

at something
i hear the devil

wears prada
but my ex

would say taco
socks let me

ruin the surprise
it gets worse

my second marriage
was an act

of god inevitable
i tell myself

even ezra needed
a *come to*

jesus moment
pound quit

imagism for
a movement he

coined vorticism
he said imagism

had lost its edge
that they waxed

fat and romantic
though ezra

really left
because amy lowell

had seized
control of his hard

light and clean
lines club which

makes me wonder
if what pound

really meant
was divorticism

if tradition
is a joke

we retell but
dont understand

FOSTER'S FREEZE

For a genealogy assignment I took a blood test. I found out I am O positive. My mom is A negative, which seems very fitting. My dad is B positive. This alone would normally frighten me. Needles should freeze in hell. I told my dad I was scared but wouldn't cry when I got pricked. He laughed, pinched my arm. Oh, positive. After this, many things became apparent.

Like, I'm adopted. That is what my teacher said. Actually she said, *You should talk to your parents.* My parents, or at least the people that identify as such, went to Hawaii last summer and brought me home a matching shirt and short set. We spoke on the phone twice while they were gone. Despite the complaints from my mom, I wore the outfit every day for two weeks until my cousin said the pattern looked like dicks exploding.

Whatever. My mom says the scheme is autumnal. And palm trees. My cousin is just jealous because her dad doesn't live with her. My mom thinks her mom is a slut, that she absolutely has patterns. They

50

are sisters. Grandma cried at Christmas after my mom saw a picture of her real dad for the first time. She was thirty. He was flexing in cutoffs next to dumbbells in prison. Oh, positive. I'm pretty sure sluts don't

get to ride on planes. My grandparents said not to talk in the movies. I've heard my uncles say that, too. Once we skipped school to watch the second *Star Wars*, then again to see *Fatal Attraction*. Oh, positive. *Davey, cover your eyes,* they said, *chichis.* An upset child can go anywhere, except a plane, my grandpa said, but he's not my blood.

I asked my mom if that made me a slut while getting dinner at Fosters Freeze. She said that wasn't polite. I'm still not sure if she meant the waitress or the sluts. My dad said men can't be sluts. Oh, positive. I sucked hard on my Twister. Looking into my straw, I saw a chunk of Snickers lodged. I tried not to cry. She said stop being silly, that I had a blood transfusion at birth. She said I was born a month late. My Rh factor is negative. My dad chewed his food and looked at his fork.

ON DREAMING OF MY WIFE

All love is a form of violence,
a domestic beat

                              in the heart
                    as much as the head, a strike to the only
thing we find vital, our safety. But that sounds so

scared, which might mean I am finally
house broken,

after all these years of really trying,
spent learning to wipe the toilet seat,
                    open the door, to provide—

    I have begun to believe my abuelita,
who believed our bodies were not built to be comfortable
            but to comfort others, as our minds

were not made for ideas
            but to catalogue groceries. I have been told
                    that love is giving orders. Last night I dreamt

    I was a feudal lord under a red pagoda heating
                    a kettle of tea with my wife.

Your own heart condemns you, I said with each sip of tea.
        I do not condemn you, she said with each sip of tea.

After waking, I felt proud,
having reached a new level of fidelity

    because she was actually in my dream.
I looked at her as a Romantic poet looks at trees.

    To think in grunts and finger points,
        admittedly, is not beyond me.

Neither is groveling. Or regret.
      These fighting techniques, I've mastered.

    Because she was naked and dangled in sleep,
        I felt horrible, knew I was,

    like it or not, intentional or not, just one man
        in a succession of men

who had stopped her from breathing
      by kissing her,
    by placing my weight atop her,
        in the name of protection.

I indicted myself, as you might indict a young couple
arguing in front of a library, neither of them dressed very well

    or looking happy because of the summer heat
        and books pinned by their elbows,

he pulling her arm, bringing her closer,

                    twisting her wrist

        when her voice ventured a little too loud, a little too far

                            beyond the yard.

DRINKING ALONE

Drinker, drinker, burning
bright, unbridled hoarse
throat, truther of the empty well, playing
follow the liter.
Sometimes
simply brewing
coffee makes rain. Starts

water
works. Uphill holds no
downpour. It is
the first. Drinking is a permanent
companion. It fixes time.

My religion,
my science, I worship rigidness. I
plan and God chuckles,

pours a drink, answers Chuy
from Boulder's plea.

Godhood hard, manhood
harder, being present not omnipresent
the hardest. Sobriety doesn't make
me a saint. Drinking isn't

my Beelzebub. Distance
is my higher power. Everyone's success
                    is an affirmation
of my failure. Looking at the moon

is time travel, peering exactly
                    one second into the past.
Achievement is the hangover of a need.

AND THREE

Look at homie, really look: a tertiary
definition of devotion. Check the
dictionary thicker than a bible open

on his desk, and it is a bible, to him,
an A to Z gospel. It takes a lot of
effort to truck paper and cardboard

bound in leather, mended with tape,
from trolley to bus, work to the gym.
And it takes a lot of effort to shift

diction. Not easy mixing registers,
at Rite Aid, scooping vanilla ice
cream, stocking boxes, or in class,

unpacking carpe diem from yolo.
It's hard to sit quietly during lecture.
Take the Greeks, their city-state

gangs, slaves, and perfection of 3's.
Homie don't see Homer in himself.
Identity is the maze's Minotaur. Helle

easy to lose yourself. It doesn't seem
like a big deal to accept Locke. Nod
at Jefferson. Academics smile when

you declare a life bent on beauty. It's
like finding God, believing you might
get a job. During Minorities in Lit,

his last elective in undergrad, the 3rd
act begins. He raises his hand and asks
when they'll read one book *about*

brown folks, if there's just one book
in his Eurocentric education that
doesn't pivot on disenfranchisement,

ain't about being less. It takes a lot of
effort to reply, *Maybe I will*, when the
professor asks, flush, *You're a poet, right?*

Why don't you write something like that?

SPORTS ANALOGY

Even if there is no I in team,
        there is damn sure a me that never fails
to get lost in a relationship,

a me that sees love as Willie Stargell saw baseball:
      a game where they give you a round bat
and throw you a round ball
           and tell you to hit it square.

    Which means love Lawrence Taylors me,
breaking me like Theismann's leg, playing

                chin music with each kiss,
submitting me with a guillotine she calls hugs,
and each conversation is a red flag the booth reviews.
      When I drop back into a relationship,

Anderson Silva cringes. Allen Iverson once asked,
          Practice?
in an interview that convinced fans he was selfish,
but I only saw a frustrated husband,
exasperated from driving around with his wife,

trying, no begging, to decide on where to eat.
        If you have a little capital
I suggest you open a restaurant called
      No Babe, You Decide.

An ex-athlete needs a place to pasture. I've come
home to so many empty apartments, half

a closet traded, that a missing couch's indention
in the carpet is team 'Tinez's logo.

A girlfriend once told me: *Stop*
hogging the rock, Hero. Get into pistols. See the ball.
          It's not five games of one on one
                 but one game of five on five.

SECOND WAVE

in this
skin i am
more wit
than man
and to
white
men i
am no
whitman
and
white women
know more
whip
than men
more
witty men
than dick—
inson
but still
not me
in this skin
i am
the white
sin of
thighs i
sin more

sway than
day or
strange than
fruit i have
picked or
night allows
more counter
space
or back
of bus
no blacks no
dogs no
mexicans
no days off
no billies just
clubs just rope
just civil
wrongs of
walking
to sit-ins
where we
all look
and grin
chicken
through
our teeth
but still
feel bit by
neither

being white
nor wit
nor man

DRAWING WATER

Picture if you will Tony Hoagland
and me, he in his *Donkey Gospel*
hat and me wearing my *Hustle* ring,
in his car patched with silver duct
tape and sagging passenger mirrors
discussing vehicles as metaphors
for systems, as waxen images of
transcendence,
      while he recklessly
          bends corners of potholed
Houston streets, clutching the
steering wheel so tightly
         as if it were the future
of American poetry. This is where
it gets complicated.
                Not complicated
as in father twists his fanny
pack as he leans forward to kiss your
forehead awkward, but just slightly
awkward because he says
             no dawg, you which
       really isn't the uncomfortable
       part. It's that we've lost
something
           between us, mostly weight,
him getting sick and me getting
  healthy. We have talked about "The

Change." He has taken one
hand off the wheel
                to gently tap my knee
and then brush up
those Van Gogh trees he
calls hair. The labyrinth
is someone's home. All men are
                part boogie. What
he tells me cannot fit in a poem,
his words no longer light enough
to lift out my chest.

HISTORY LESSON

I imagined us a nation
because our house
was our corner of the world.

Of course, it was
your house, and my world.

Remember when those two
large paintings arrived?

I was so scared. Inside
those boxes were all your
conspiracies. How secretive

I was, agent against history,
the newest New Yorker

in New Mexico, revolting
against a past that wasn't

mine, scoffing at Santa Fe,
struggling to understand
its dust, so unimpressed
by its art collectors and its

architecture. It's hard to
hike in Hender Scheme,
not to scuff heels

in hills. What's in the attic
but a vacuum-packed
subconscious, a few

moldy berries of memory,
a few buried Members Only
jackets. Let us not keep
the cellar full of boxes

untouched. Let us not keep
the paintings of Indians hidden.

FRACTAL

the second time
i was married
it was after three
weeks of drinking
wine chased
by hurricanes she
is so damn hot
i thought i mean
warm & exotic
so damn loving
i said inside the
eye of a storm
light refracts turns
every thing upside
down marriage is
a natural disaster
a speakeasy is
no different than
a watering hole
it propagates the
species because
so much of nature
stays exposed
we cover ourselves
initially love is a test
of vision trying to
love someone in

to loving you
we call this sight
we calm this sight
we call it serenity
carpe diem i do
everything like it
is the first time
when coupled i am
both the night owl
& the plucked fowl
with perfect vision
i can see myself
courting hitched like
talons to a mouse

FOOTNOTING BIGGIE LYRICS LIKE *WHY CHRISTMAS MISSED US*

When I was just a snot nose
      is one of my favorite
      demotic phrases,
                 for its fealty to two lords
that fickle balance of sound
and meaning
that is part air
          and part earth—as much head
      as heart, which relies on a metonymy
we all recognize
         as tied to vulgarity
                and transcendence
dependent upon our ability
             to be vulnerable again.

1) I *recognize a real Don when I see one*
         as you know your child's head
      shaved, braided, or pomaded with dried soda.
      I find it remarkable that I can spot my car

amongst its honeycomb of plastic and glass
         or that I don't walk out a restaurant
with someone's black jacket more often. We identify

      inanimate objects when we find
            contiguity within them
because we see possessions

as extensions of ourselves. There is a slaver
 inside me yet.

 Real recognizes Real, which
 is why the eyes of mammals look familiar,
 and the eyes of insects don't,

why we gas roaches, smash spiders, annihilate ants,
why I recognized the line of NOTORIOUS B.I.G.
 Remember when we used to eat sardines for dinner

 not because I ate sardines for dinner—more like
chili spaghetti, chipped beef,

occasionally pot roast, anything my mom,
 being a single mom of two, could make
quickly and cheaply after work,
 while my brother and I watched.

2) Biggie didn't teach me to cook,
though his "Ten Crack Commandments"

 did instruct
 how to move weight, flip birds,
 be a dope boy. This is how

 my mother taught me to cook,
 or more aptly,
tricked me how to cook. First, she left

                              a fully prepared roast
                    in the fridge and a note on the oven
                    with a specific temperature and time.

The next time she asked me to prepare
the carrots,
                              then it was carrots
                              and potatoes.
She was always crafty, in that way.
                    My first *talk* wasn't
the birds and the bees but carrots and potatoes.

                    She requested easy dishes
I had watched her make for years. I complained
but cooked
                              not because I loved her
                              but because I was hungry. I was 12.

I was always hungry. I'm still hungry.
          At 19, I loved the music of Biggie,

                              but I still didn't love
my mother. I was darker in thought than now. I mean,
                    all my friends were black. I mean,

I thought I was black. I mean, I wanted
                                        to be black
                    because I was crosshatched,

stuck between the earth and the air,
caught in a pickle, jumped from the frying
pan to the fire,

called the kettle black, had a complex complexion,
because all I could do was injure my own injin's engine.

A KISS

And sometimes it is
loss

          that we lose,

    and sometimes

it is just lips. When I was

       a child, I would ask my mother
to tuck me in,

         wrap me tight in blankets,

    make me into a burrito.

       Sometimes I would wait in bed,

pressing my body stiff like a board,

mind like a feather, silly—setting the scene

     to be seen.

        So I could be wrapped.

        So I could be kissed.

And what

               I miss most,

is being   made   . again.

FLIGHT OF LOVE

Not in the beginning   but near the end,

        it must have been
                    a maniacally

perfect god   that made   the heart,

that would make men,
        men   and   women, women,
with nothing in particular   but spare

      parts:

Judge me not

                  for always being enameled
                      in love, painted
in a relationship. Let the first ones without sex

          get stoned. On *Maury*
one sister chastises another for naming her children

after cars
           she'll never own. On telenovelas dark

skinned maids make the sign of the cross
after buttoning their blouses.

                    We double-check our doors
        are locked in the city of Love. El Diablo
        was once called "On-Hell."
                            My hat wears a haloed A.

Her velour butt is struck
                    by Cupid's sequined arrow.
        We are angels in our way.

                    What is love but a tongue
        taught to us by our grandmothers,
                    brought to us from their shores.

No matter how many times I put
sexuality in the corner,

            put gender in a pantsuit
and call it Diane Keaton, I cannot forget
my father's straw sayings, his broken camel back,

his sparrow-winged shoulders straightened
                    from saying nothing. *I am a man,*
                        said silence.

I sit on a plane, shifting in my seat, wanting
to take off my shoes,

and try to talk to the person next to me.
I am constantly trying to talk
to the person next to me.

Usually the person next to me is someone I love.
Normally I won't know them. In the Bible
to have relations with a woman
is to know her.

A fork can't escape
the discourse of its

drawer, as a lover
can't escape being

the big spoon.
Let us staycation
in the attainable.

We call our sleep
routine the Kama
Sleeptra.

Every night, in
bed, she says,
*You know what to
do. Seahorse.* The

difference between
simile and metaphor
is liking and loving.

Sleeping, like loving,
is a solitary act
done in complicity.

*You're my doll.
I know how
to arrange you.
Whatever it takes.*

What yo-yos we are,
lovers of intimate distance

swung together by
twine   and time,

near the same   flame. The door that opened

Agathon

next to Socrates

made   Plato fondle   his pen

to tell us that

it was what god

intended,

independent

of parts,   that we lay upon

each other.

THE ART OF THE VIGILANTE

Something there is that loves
a mask, needs darkness, yearns
for a muzzle and blindness,
the silence of zip ties. Some walls

love the cold, wind Minutemen
to soldier along the border, celebrate the Alamo,
the thwarting of the Plan de San Diego, *Niña*, *Pinta*,
Santa Maria, memorize the year 1492.

Animus is a prickly
pear, lines gelatin powder in women's underwear,
connects my father to a Mexican mother
land, convinces him
to make America great again. Some things

have zero chill. Where are we, güey, that rivers turn
red, and the dead's tongues dry blue. Under stars
we scab together
like saguaros in the desert.

There weren't enough Spaniards
to fuck the Indian out of us.
Out of you.
There is no flower   that su-
stains the field.

When will we wade out of hate?
Speaking from behind sheets, galloping on horseback

        with noose in hand, our notions swing in the breeze.
My consciousness is a cut eyehole.

So, galloping on what others have said and thought, yelling,
we circle a rancho and burn it down, and move on to the next, silent.

AND FOUR

is also, besides a step, a cry, 4, warning
golfers of an errant shot. Unfortunate
telling. A searching and fearless moral
inventory, a poem, is a place to isolate,

hack in stone. 4. Real drunks orpheus
their addiction. Homie misses the ritual,
mostly, passing the horn around a fire.
His tribe's gotten smaller. The game's

the game, they say. His student loans
descend, ominously, like frogs from
heaven. Weight won't wait. In African
myth, growing wings typifies unease.

Look at Homie on the beach picking
shells in dress shoes, wondering why
he chose poetry. Look at Homie siting
on a bed in Monterey Bay, black suit

and tie, intent on fishing the finish
of a bottle, promising to stop drinking
                    while drinking.
Homie left without leaving the room.

FOUND FRAGMENT ON AMBITION

v.

if a hood is a sense of place
& a sense of place is identity
then identity is a hood & adult
hood is being insecure in any
hood a hood scares the whitest
folks why folks scared to stop
in the hood & why folks stop
wearing a hood & call it white
nationalism if i tried i would
fail to pass if i failed i would
try to pass when can i retire my
bowl stop needing to beg for my
person hood you see academically
my ghetto pass was revoked please
sir can you direct me to the window
to turn in my man card where
can i apply to enter the whiteness
protection program ive lost
my found identity is a hood
a hood is a sense of place
a place places a hood hood in us

PLAYING HANGMAN

I have read through enough of the Bible
  Belt, the Rust Belt, down Appalachia,

all across Los Angeles, Carbondale, Louisville,
  through enough extended stretches

  of Texas, alone,
under lightning from clouds at half
  mast, played hangman
      in the marginalia

of lit magazines
with enough freshmen shrugged

off to college, a box of books
  for at-risk teens orphaned
      beneath my feet,

    to know
    family is not forever.

Smiles and hellos
go a long way on the road
to saying goodbye. Often

    a poet's only grandeur
    is a faux-leather seat

connected to sloshes of internet. I am hung
up

on so much. On a Megabus
there is nothing more tragic

than a boy with headphones
singing
next to my seat by the restroom. Eighty
miles later and I still *Superman*

them hoes. Eventually you become
your penetralia, your addictions,

even if it's diction. I've become the patron
saint of high school seniors sentenced

to poetry. I am the poet laureate of angst.
Call me Subordinate Claus,

ho ho hum.

On my way home from Houston,
I watch as a young couple

climb down the upper deck. This young
man sports the same fade as my eldest son,

the same wonder razored
in his head. *Bitch, you can skirt,*

ya dig?
said the young man typed
                    to life.
He is the color of my desertion.
She is the shade of expectations thrown.

                    It is deeply ingrained
                    that things are wrong

with me. So I blame
the fates that I travel far, that I live young

     to die old, that I
confuse my experience
for loose change in a mother's purse.

              When playing Words With
              Friends with my sons

     we never spell out *absent.*
I tell you what's wrong with me
because I love you.

               This young man
reminded me that to skirt means leave
       and when one skirts from a skirt,

an odyssey embarks. Not from shadow
       but into shadow does the animal
       of the mind leap, and I have miles to go,

thin walls to hold,

and cages to keep.

We hang from what makes us great.

ACKNOWLEDGMENTS

Academy of American Poets' *Poem-a-Day*, "A Kiss," and
"The/A Train"

American Poetry Review, "And One," "And Two," "Falling," "After
Imagism," "Drinking Alone," "Found Fragment on Ambition,"
"Playing Hangman," and "Dedication"

Boston Review, "Footnoting Biggie Lyrics Like *Why Christmas
Missed Us*"

Crab Orchard Review, "Allegedly Hemingway Wrote Drunk"

LitHub, "They Call Him Scarface Because He's Sad"

Orion, "Fractal"

Oxford American, "In Defence of Poetry Voice"

Pleiades, "On Dreaming of My Wife"

Poetry Foundation's *PoetryNow*, "Us vs Them"

Poetry International, "And Four"

Poetry Magazine, "Consider Oedipus' Father" and "Love Song"

Prairie Schooner, "Sports Analogy"

Pushcart Prize XLII, edited by Bill Henderson (Pushcart Press, 2017),
"Consider Oedipus' Father"

Sporklet, "Hoodies" and "Second Wave"

Tin House, "Hexaptych on Ambition" (published as "Triptych on
Ambition")

Sections of poems first published in:
*Crab Orchard Review, Hyperallergic, The Journal, Los Angeles Review of
Books, Lumina Journal, Ploughshares*, and *Verse Junkies*.

All respect, all love, all light to Juan Felipe Herrera, Vievee Francis, Ilya Kaminsky, Adrian Matejka, Tony Hoagland, Kevin Prufer, Eduardo C. Corral, Natalie Diaz, Luis Urrea, Gabrielle Calvocoressi, A. Van Jordan, Gregory Pardlo, francine j. harris, Lacy Johnson, Martha Serpas, Yusef Komunyakaa, Tarfia Faizullah, Matthew Olzmann, Jamaal May, Mat Johnson, Robert Boswell, David Rivard, Tom Sleigh, Stuart Dischell, Tomás Q. Morín, Matthew Zapruder, Maria Gonzalez, Curtis Bauer, John Poch, Wendy Xu, Jess Smith, Chen Chen, Jess Grover, Rosebud Ben-Oni, Darrel Alejandro Holnes, Sandra Alcosser, Tess Taylor, Elizabeth Scanlon, Glover Davis, Kaveh Akbar, Jeff Shotts, Timothy Donnelly, Don Share, Rigoberto González, Major Jackson, Rachel Eliza Griffiths, Kristen Radtke, Kristen Miller, Ariel Lewiton, Jeffrey Skinner, Sarah Gorham, Mom, Dad, Mark, Anthony, Isiah, and Xochi.

Biggest thanks and abrazos to Kelsy Yates for her support and love; without her, none of this would be possible.

Thank you to Bread Loaf and CantoMundo for fellowships. Love to San Diego State University. Thank you to Texas Tech University for a visiting assistant professorship for the 2015–2016 academic year. Thank you to Columbia University. Thank you to the National Endowment for the Arts for a 2017 grant.

DEDICATION

Lately,
I sleep

most hours
of the day,

not because
I'm depressed,

but so as not
to give up
on my dreams.

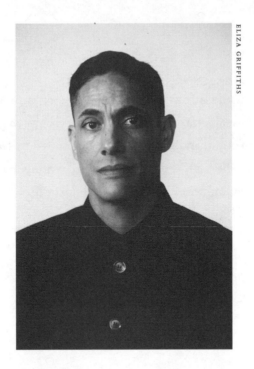

ELIZA GRIFFITHS

DAVID TOMAS MARTINEZ is a CantoMundo fellow and recipient of a 2017 NEA Fellowship, a Pushcart Prize, the Inprint Paul Verlaine Prize in Poetry, and the Stanley P. Young Fellowship from Bread Loaf. *Hustle*, his debut collection from Sarabande, won the New England Book Festival's Poetry Prize, the Devil's Kitchen Reading Award, and $10,000 from the Alfredo Cisneros Del Moral Foundation. Poems from the new book have appeared in *Tin House*, *Oxford American*, *Boston Review*, *Prairie Schooner*, *Ploughshares*, and *Poetry*. He lives in Brooklyn.

SARABANDE BOOKS is a nonprofit literary press located in Louisville, KY. Founded in 1994 to champion poetry, short fiction, and essay, we are committed to creating lasting editions that honor exceptional writing. For more information, please visit sarabandebooks.org.